CUMBRIAN TRACTION

Gordon Edgar

AMBERLEY

Front cover: By the time that the 2T20 Carlisle–Sellafield 'Workers' Commuter Train' trial service made an appearance at Nethertown on the Cumbrian Coast Line at 7.40 a.m. on 15 February 2012, the sun had risen and the cloud cover had significantly increased, but there was the benefit of pleasing subtle tones in the sky. Indeed, at this time of the morning the sun would have been insufficiently high to illuminate the train and foreground. Direct Rail Services (DRS) Class 37/4 37423 *Spirit of the Lakes* was in charge of the trial service during its final week of operation and the train makes an impressive sight powering through Nethertown station alongside the coastline, with St Bees Head in the background.

Rear cover: Observing the mandatory 20 mph speed restriction, the driver of DRS 37603 and 37602 eases his reasonable trailing load of five flasks across the recently fully renovated viaduct at Harrington on 28 April 2011, heading the diverted 6C53 Crewe–Sellafield flask working.

First published 2014

Amberley Publishing
The Hill, Stroud
Gloucestershire, GL5 4EP

www.amberley-books.com

Copyright © Gordon Edgar, 2014

The right of Gordon Edgar to be identified as
the Author of this work has been asserted in
accordance with the Copyrights, Designs and
Patents Act 1988.

ISBN 978 1 4456 3938 3 (print)
ISBN 978 1 4456 3950 5 (ebook)

British Library Cataloguing in Publication Data.
A catalogue record for this book is available from
the British Library.

Typesetting by Amberley Publishing.
Printed in the UK.

Introduction

Cumbria offers a rich tapestry of scenery, types of rail route and colourful traction, ranging from vintage Type 1 diesels first introduced under the British Railways (BR) Modernisation Scheme in the late 1950s, through to the latest locomotive to be introduced to the national network, namely the Direct Rail Services (DRS) Class 68 'Eurolight' 3,750 hp diesel locomotive. There is no other county in the country offering such a diversity of topography and locomotive types; it is hardly unsurprising that the railways of Cumbria continue to draw the follower of railways like a magnet, much as they have done for many years. In fact, most of the routes in the county are now as busy as ever since the years leading up to the demise of steam traction on BR.

The principal north–south route, the West Coast Main Line (WCML), runs approximately up the spine of the county over the well-known Shap summit, flanked to the west by the stunning Cumbrian Coast route and to the east by the renowned Settle and Carlisle line (S&C), the subject of much world-wide acclaim since its threatened closure in the 1980s, well after Dr Beeching's rationalisation of the UK network had made its mark on some of the county's routes. A section of the delightful Tyne Valley route, running through 'Hadrian's Wall Country', also falls within the county boundary, and the border between England and Scotland is crossed by means of the little-known Sark river bridge at Gretna Green. In effect, the rail routes of the county are bounded by Mossband in the north, Gilsland in the east, Burton-in-Kendal in the south-west on the WCML, and Ais Gill summit in the south-east on the S&C line. And not forgetting the westernmost point of any railway in the county, at St Bees on the Cumbrian Coast line. Consequently, the fine backdrops of the Lakeland Fells and Northern Pennines are never too far away from any of the routes around the county, all so diverse in character and offering both the rail traveller and photographer pleasing scenes at any time of the year.

The Border City of Carlisle continues to be a focal point for the many charters visiting the present day county town (Penrith originally holding this title), attracting all manner of locomotive types, both of heritage and contemporary design. The splendid Grade II-listed and one-time joint railway company station, initially constructed in 1847 and standing alongside the city's Citadel, must rank as one of the finest of the principal through stations in the country, despite serving a city of a relatively modest population – an indication of the strategic importance of the complex intersection of rail routes converging on the city, two of which, the Waverley and Silloth lines, sadly are no longer with us today.

Industry within the county is a stark shadow of its former self, particularly with the contraction of traditional industries once located in the West Cumbrian district, which included coal mining and steel manufacture. However, a number of railfreight interfaces still provide facilities for an appreciable volume of freight traffic in the county, most notably those serving the Sellafield Reprocessing Plant, the timber felled in the Kielder Forest district, petroleum and bulk cement deliveries on the outskirts of Carlisle and the quarried products around the Shap area. The high level of Anglo-Scottish rail traffic, in particular containerised consumables and imported coal, ensure that the strategic freight paths over the WCML and S&C routes are keenly sought after by the various freight operating companies which use the county rail network. In particular, DRS has gone from strength to strength, from its initial humble beginnings with some nuclear flask traffic and the occasional modest railfreight trials during the early days of privatisation in the late 1990s to offering a broad portfolio of freight and passenger operations. The company's incredibly varied fleet of locomotives, specially chosen to offer maximum network route availability to its now broad range of customers, continues to grow in number and diversity, undoubtedly perpetuating Carlisle and the greater county as a 'hot spot' for observers of the contemporary railway scene. In fact, the establishment of Kingmoor TMD as the company's main traction maintenance depot and head office after the company took over the derelict site in 1998 was an extremely shrewd move, providing DRS with both a strategic and an enviable location on the railway network.

The collection of photographs brought together in this book have all been taken by the author and cover the period from the early days of privatisation through to 2014, including the much anticipated arrival of DRS' new Class 68 mixed-traffic locomotive. They have been specially chosen to portray the incredible cross-section of locomotive types, liveries and network diagrams, both passenger and freight, for which they operate. The diversity of the landscape and the broad climate range in which they can be seen in action has also not been overlooked when making this selection, which it is to be hoped will give the reader an overview of almost the last two decades of Cumbrian Traction.

Gordon Edgar, Carlisle
March 2014

Opposite: There was a milestone event for DRS on 28 July 1997; it was the first day that their first newly acquired Class 37/6 locomotives were used in revenue-earning service. 20303 (with 20304 out of view) stands in Penrith down sidings, having brought the empty 'Piggyback' semi-trailer overnight from Cricklewood. 37609 (with temporary DRS decals and Tankfreight body side logos) and 37610 (still with the EPS 'Nightstar' circles) prepare to set back onto the main line with the loaded tank, forming the afternoon service to Cricklewood. Just one prototype 'Piggyback' tanker was built and certified by Derby RTC for network use, funded out of Tankfreight's annual development budget, in order to trial the concept. The trial was an absolute operational success and would have been financially viable long-term as a block train service; however the customer, Milk Marque, was disbanded by the government-led Monopolies & Mergers Commission, sadly bringing to an end the prospect of milk transport returning to rail.

DRS Class 20/3s 20303 and 20304 with a 'Piggyback' semi-trailer loaded on a Tiphook Rail swing well pocket wagon at Penrith on 19 July 1997. The 30,000 litres of milk, collected by a smaller farm collection vehicle and reloaded at the siding, would be delivered that evening to the Cricklewood railhead and then taken on by road to the Chadwell Heath Dairy in London. DRS Driver William Walsh sets back onto the main line from the down sidings under the supervision of Alan Ramshay from the DRS Engineering Department. The author was Tankfreight's project manager for this 'Piggyback' concept and this proving trial on behalf of Milk Marque ran for twenty-eight consecutive days.

On 27 August 2002, DRS *Crompton*, 33030, stands on the precise alignment of the former Waverley Line at the Kingstown railhead of Carlisle Warehousing Ltd during a trial of the Minimodal 2.5m container concept, just prior to returning to Carlisle yard and Kingmoor depot. Four of the containers are already loaded on the Malcolm semi-trailer alongside. This was the first of two days of operational trials and filming prior to the official concept launch at the National Railway Museum in September of that year.

Upon joining DRS in 2002, one of the author's first projects was to manage the Minimodal trials as well as the filming and its launch at the National Railway Museum. A short professional filming sequence, with the cooperation of Network Rail, Royal Mail and Virgin Trains, was undertaken at Carlisle station shortly after first light on 28 August 2002, prior to further footage being taken on the Settle–Carlisle line. The intermodal concept was a Strategic Rail Authority Innovation Award winner in 2000; the lightweight cube containers had a 'W6A' loading gauge classification and could go anywhere on the National Network when carried on the Megafret-type intermodal wagon as seen here. The roller-shutter doors allowed easy access at station platforms and the whole unit could be lifted with a heavy-duty forklift truck at terminals or yards for road distribution if required. The system did not progress any further than this short trial with DRS, and the Royal Mail moved to road distribution shortly after this. DRS Crompton Class 33 No. 33025 (with 33030 on the rear) stands in Carlisle station's platform 3 as the Royal Mail loading/unloading operation and filming takes place.

Above: Freightliner Heavyhaul 66607 sets back onto its train of empty PCA four-wheel cement tanks at Stainton Junction, the truncated remains of the former North British Railway Waverley Line out of Carlisle. This short branch, accessed from Carlisle yard (from the right) to Brunthill sidings at Kingstown (to the left), is all that remains of the southern section of the Waverley Line and had been mothballed for over a year since the steel products conveyed for Metal Box Ltd by DB Schenker (DBS) had ceased. This was the first of the irregular bulk and bagged cement services by rail to Carlisle from Oxwellmains cement works near Dunbar, on a very wet 22 June 2012. The erstwhile Carlisle Canal steam motive power depot was located on the bank high above the River Eden, in the background of this view.

Below: DRS 33025 (still with its Minimodal decals) and 20302 skirt the Irish Sea at Parton on Saturday 9 August 2003, heading the Sellafield–Kingmoor Yard empty caustic soda tanks, destined for Ineos Chlor at Runcorn.

The outward 2T20 06.15 Carlisle–Sellafield and Barrow DRS trial service was not an easy working to capture in conventional light at this time of the year. The temperature on this morning was -3°C, with frost on the sedge and a biting easterly wind. DRS Class 47/8 No. 47810 *Peter Bath MBE 1927–2006* crosses the Eskmeals Viaduct between Ravenglass and Bootle at 8.10 a.m. on 8 February 2012. The sun had still not risen above the Cumbrian Fells, but the wonderful subtle tones evident at this time of the morning were sufficient to produce a result.

This was the penultimate week of the DRS 'Sellafield Workers' Train' trial. The sun disappeared during the early afternoon behind a thin veil of cloud, and the temperature during the day did not increase much above freezing. The remaining diffused light for the 4.45 p.m. departure from Sellafield, with a 'wrong-side' viewpoint, allowed the incorporation of the far more pleasing coastal scene between Nethertown and Braystones. DRS Class 37/4 No. 37423 *Spirit of the Lakes* has just got into its stride heading the 2T21 Sellafield–Carlisle service on 8 February 2012, seemingly conveying more rail enthusiasts than prospective regular commuters from Sellafield.

The 6Z68 Killoch–Cottam Freightliner Heavyhaul loaded with coal hoppers, which subsequently took the Settle and Carlisle route, crosses an incredibly still River Esk at Mossband on 6 February 2012 with 70013 confidently in charge.

It is dawn alongside the Cumbrian Coast line at Nethertown on 15 February 2012 and the trial Carlisle–Sellafield 'Workers' Commuter Train' is running on this day. The distinctive growl of a Class 37 working extremely hard is heard in the direction of St Bees, but a quick check of the watch suggested that this could not be the passenger service. To the author's delight a well-loaded Carlisle Yard–Sellafield acid tank service, with DRS 37087 *Keighley & Worth Valley Railway 40th Anniversary 1968–2008* in charge, rounded the curve and powered through Nethertown station at 7.23 a.m. Seventeen minutes later there was the spectacle of yet another Class 37 working, on a passenger train, as depicted on the front cover. Was this really 2012 or was it merely a dream?

The sun dips into the horizon over the Solway Firth behind the photographer as a seasonal extra of empty container flat wagons desperately required in Scotland – the 4S61 Crewe Basford Hall–Coatbridge 'additional working' with Freightliner's 86622 and 86627 in charge – scream across the Esk River Bridge at Mossband near Gretna on Thursday 13 December 2012.

Running over three hours behind its booked path, the 6Z88 Doncaster Belmont Yard–New Cumnock empty coal in 'MEA' wagons, with ex-works DB Schenker 'super Tug' No. 60059 *Swinden Dalesman* in charge, was captured crossing the Eden river bridge in a rare burst of sunshine on Tuesday 20 November 2012. The crew change was carried out at Carlisle station instead of at the New Yard; hence the working was unusually routed via the down fast out of the Border City. This unusual working offered followers in Scotland the rare opportunity of a visit by a Class 60 north of the border.

Above: DBS 92009 *Elgar* briskly crosses the Eden river bridge in charge of the 4M63 Mossend–Hams Hall intermodal on 18 March 2011.

Below: The new and old Freightliner corporate liveries are seen, carried by 86622 and 86613 respectively, heading the 4M74 Coatbridge–Crewe intermodal across the Esk river bridge at Mossband shortly before sunset on 8 April 2011.

The time-honoured tradition of handing over a prestigious locomotive-hauled service can still occasionally be witnessed at Carlisle station. DRS Kingmoor driver Mike Wylie has just brought in the 1Z48 *Northern Belle* charter train from Edinburgh, as Driver Ian Munroe of Crewe depot clambers aboard the footplate to take the service forward to Manchester Victoria. The railfan further down the platform adds the final finishing touch to this timeless scene. DRS 47805 made a tremendous sound as it departed into the night, right on time; not bad for a locomotive almost fifty years old.

A positive feast of traction at Carlisle station! Virgin Trains Class 87 *The Black Prince* leaves Carlisle propelling a Glasgow–Euston service, while stabled under the station's fine overall roof are 90020, 47810, 57320 and 47841. This was 22 February 2004, a weekend when Anglo-Scottish West Coast services were diverted via the Glasgow & South Western route through Kilmarnock, with diesel locomotives performing 'drags' of the electric locomotives and coaching stock.

Virgin Trains Class 87 No. 87024 *Lord of the Isles* stands at Carlisle heading a Euston–Glasgow service on 22 February 2004, with 47841 stabled in one of the centre roads.

No. 87002 *Royal Sovereign* propels the empty stock from the 1Z86 London Euston–Carlisle 'Cumbrian Mountain Express' to the shunt neck at Carlisle South Junction on Saturday 9 March 2013. The *Electric Scot* locomotive was used to retain train heating for the stock of the steam-hauled charter while at Carlisle, as well as to clear platform 3 at Carlisle for other services.

Europhoenix Ltd-owned Class 86/7s 86701 *Orion* and 86702 *Cassiopeia*, bearing the striking Electric Traction Ltd livery and engaged in overnight ice clearance duties, are stabled alongside Carlisle station on 3 December 2010. The British Rail Class 86 was the standard electric locomotive built during the 1960s, developed as a result of testing with the earlier classes 81, 82, 83, 84 and 85. One hundred of these locomotives were built from 1965–1966 by either English Electric at Vulcan Foundry, Newton-le-Willows, or British Rail at their Doncaster works. The class was built to haul trains on the then newly electrified West Coast Main Line, from London Euston to Birmingham, Crewe, Manchester Piccadilly, Liverpool and later Preston, Carlisle and Glasgow. They helped to replace steam locomotives, which were finally withdrawn by BR in 1968. 86701, delivered new from Doncaster in December 1965, originally carried the number E3129 and is now in Colas Freight colours. 86702 bore the number E3144 when delivered from the Vulcan Foundry in March 1966.

Former West Coast Main Line stalwarts, AC electric traction used for ice clearance duties during the winter period. 86101 *Sir William A Stanier FRS*, 86702 and 86701 at Carlisle station on 9 December 2010.

After some quite intensive overnight use during the 2012/13 winter season, the *Ice Maiden* AC electrics 86101 and 87002 took on a satisfying retro 'work-worn' appearance. On 11 March 2013. and just before their journey back south, to an uncertain future on the UK national network, they stand in the falling snow at Carlisle station.

On Saturday 24 August 2013, Freightliner Intermodal 86613 and 86612 pass through Carlisle station heading the 4M01 Coatbridge–Crewe Basford Hall, with disgraced 90043 *Freightliner Coatbridge* standing on the down centre road, having failed on a northbound service some days previously.

A diverted Aberdeen–Kings Cross service, with East Coast HST power car 43302 leading, departing from Carlisle on 11 September 2010.

The diverted 1E11 07.52 Aberdeen–London King's Cross gets underway from Carlisle on 9 November 2013, with HST power car 43367 *Deltic 50 – 1955–2005* on the rear.

Carlisle Citadel station was designed by Sir William Tite in 1847 and is a Grade II listed structure, including the rather fine curved footbridge, an integral part of the overall Tudor style adopted for the station by Tite, who was architect to the Caledonian Railway. This station served an unusually large number of railway companies, though it was built by only two of them jointly, the Caledonian and the Lancaster & Carlisle. Others were the North British, the Midland, the North Eastern, the Glasgow & South Western, and the Maryport & Carlisle. The station therefore experienced periodic expansion from the original; however, much of the building remains little altered to this day. DRS 66431 passes beneath the arched footbridge heading the 4M44 Coatbridge–Daventry Malcolm intermodal on Tuesday 17 September 2013.

Network Rail's 'New Measurement Train' (NMT) crosses the River Eden with HST Class 43 power car No. 43062 *John Armitt* leading, the 1Q26 Derby Railway Technical Centre–Glasgow Central on 27 March 2012. The NMT, launched in 2003, is a specialised train which assesses the condition of track so that engineers can subsequently determine where to work. The train measures the contact between rails, wheels and the overhead electric supply line. Lasers and other instruments are used to make other measurements of the track geometry and other features such as overhead line height and stagger, and the track gauge, twist and cant. On the West Coast Main Line, particular care has to be taken to ensure that clearances are maintained for the use of tilting trains. The train captures video footage from the front and rear power cars, and video of the pantograph and wheel interfaces.

Following a night and almost full day of continuously heavy rainfall, the River Esk at Mossband is looking fierce as 'AL6' Class 86 AC electric E3137/86259 crosses heading the 5Z86 empty stock move from Edinburgh Waverley–Southall on Monday 5 August 2013.

86101 *Sir William A Stanier FRS* heads the 1Z86 Watford–Edinburgh Rail-Blue charter near Southwaite on 6 May 2011.

It is rare to see electric traction at the head of petroleum tankers but happily these were just empties being returned to the refinery. DBS 92037 *Sullivan* heads the 6S36 Dalston–Grangemouth Refinery empties near Floriston crossing on 25 September 2010, the Class 92 having replaced a Class 66 in Kingmoor Yard.

There's no snoozing on this Caledonian sleeper train; the hapless passengers of the 1S26 London Euston–Glasgow on Friday 2 August 2013 had a rude awakening, not in Glasgow as expected, but Preston at 6.27 a.m., and were asked to continue their journey in a more conventional manner. The service was delayed, due firstly to a network issue in the Tring area, and then a problem with one of the coaches. By the time it reached Preston, 168 minutes late, a decision was taken to terminate the service and de-train the undoubtedly disgruntled and bleary-eyed passengers. This is the empty stock move, the 5S26 07.58 Preston–Polmadie crossing the Eden river bridge at Carlisle, providing this rare daylight opportunity in Cumbria.

The mist quickly rolls in with the tide on the River Esk from the Solway Firth as the 3Q73 Carlisle Wapping Sidings–Mossend test train rolls by with Class 31 No. 31602 *Driver Dave Green* propelling the ensemble of Network Rail-liveried stock on 6 February 2012.

The 1Z89 Motherwell–Carmarthen Six Nations Rugby charter stands in platform 3 at Carlisle in the unusual combination of sun and falling snow, and almost three hours late. Disgraced DRS 47501 *Craftsman* leading was about to be removed from the train, the driver standing under the canopy to the left, leaving 47818, piloted by 57007 and 57010, to take the train forward to the Principality.

Prior to taking a Carlisle Yard–Crewe Basford Hall sleeper carrier on Sunday 23 June 2013, Colas Rail 47739 *Robin of Templecombe 1938–2013* and 56087 are seen stabled alongside Carlisle station's west retaining wall. 56087 was declared a failure working northbound empty timber wagons from Chirk on the previous Wednesday and was being returned to depot for repair.

On 28 March 2012, DBS 66091 skirts the River Caldew in Cummersdale, heading the 6S36 Dalston–Grangemouth empty BP petroleum tankers. A further six tanks, shuttled earlier in the morning, would be attached to this portion at Carlisle Yard before the service proceeded to the Grangemouth Refinery.

Just before sunrise on 28 March 2012, DRS 66423 drags 37423, two nuclear flasks collected from Torness power station during the previous day and a twin-deck container carrier, forming the 6C22 6.45 a.m. Kingmoor DRS Depot–Sellafield service, passing the Stead McAlpin textile mill in Cummersdale. The company provided the textiles that fitted out the saloon in the RMS *Titanic* and Queen Victoria's yacht and the exact fabric designs are now being reprinted again at this mill.

Providing a reminder of previous everyday traction on the route, Network Rail 'skinhead' Class 31/1 31106 glints in the low evening sun heading the 3Q20 7.58 p.m. Carlisle High Wapping–Derby RTC at Howe & Co. Sidings, Cotehill, on the Settle and Carlisle line on 20 May 2011.

DRS' unique Stobart-liveried Class 66/4 No. 66411 *Eddie the Engine* heading the Mossend–Daventry 'Tesco Express' during its brief pause for a crew change at Carlisle on a wet 13 January 2009. This Class 66/4 locomotive was subsequently stripped of its decals and handed back to the leasing company, Lloyds Bank Leasing Group. Freightliner subsequently took on a lease and transferred it to Poland for use there.

A book on Cumbrian Traction would be incomplete without one of the magnificent Solway sunsets featuring. On 13 August 2003, an unidentified EWS Class 90 speeds across the Esk river bridge at Mossband in charge of a Willesden–Shieldmuir postal service, just two months after the Royal Mail had announced that it was to withdraw its entire network of rail services for mail distribution by March 2004, in favour of a road-based distribution network.

Above: Following completion of another 'Jacobite' season on the West Highland extension line, West Coast Railway Co. (WCRC) Class 37 No. 37518 *Fort William*, still bearing its heritage railways guise of the Intercity 'Swallow' livery, pilots Peppercorn K1 2-6-0 No. 62005 through Carlisle station, the 5Z52 8.34 a.m. Fort William–Carnforth loco move on Saturday 26 October 2013. The Class 37 was to receive its WCRC corporate livery soon after acquisition by the Carnforth-based operator.

Below: During the late evening of Friday 11 May 2012, Carlisle station was graced with the Stratford Class 47 Group's large logo blue 47580 *County of Essex*. The ex-Stratford Class 47 is seen here waiting for the road to Dumfries heading the return Compass Tours 'Heart of Wales Explorer' charter, the 1Z43 Cardiff Central–Dumfries. Introduced to BR service on 1 September 1964 as D1762, she was first allocated to 41A Tinsley depot, and has been in preservation since 2007.

The combination of the late-running 6C42 acid tanks from Sellafield to Kingmoor and the early running OM44 Seaton–Sellafield (with a crew change at Carlisle station instead of, as usual, at Bog Junction) provided the unusual sight of DRS traction dominance on the west side of Carlisle station on 14 May 2012. 37423 *Spirit of the Lakes* was heading for Kingmoor depot with the acid tanks (which would be taken on to Middlesbrough as the 6E44 later in the afternoon behind 37612), as 57002 and 57011 wait for the road to Sellafield following a crew change.

DRS 47790 *Galloway Princess* on an Edinburgh–London Euston 'Northern Belle' duty at Carlisle station on 20 August 2012. Delivered new from BR Crewe Works to Haymarket (64B) depot as D1973 in November 1965, it was subsequently identified as 47272, 47593, 47673, 47790, 47593 and finally back to 47790! However, it has carried just three names: *Galloway Princess*, *York InterCity Control* and *Saint David/Dewi Sant*. It was acquired by DRS from DBS in March 2007 and its first name, originally applied in 1983, was rededicated by DRS in July 2009, and renumbering back to 47790 quickly followed.

Making a return to their former home city, HN Rail's pair of ex-DRS Class 20s, 20311 and 20314, top and tail a pair of barrier coaches through Carlisle station, the 5Z20 Washwood Heath–Wabtec Kilmarnock, for the collection of refurbished First Great Western vehicles on 21 August 2012, and just before the last of the evening sunlight disappeared.

DRS 20309 and 20303 have a reasonable trailing load on this diverted 6K73 Sellafield–Crewe at Blackwell Hall on 31 May 2011.

Above: DRS 20303 and 20309 head the 6M22 Hunterston–Kingmoor flasks across the River Esk bridge at Mossband on 26 May 2011.

Below: The same DRS Class 20 duo, 20303 and 20309, approach Whitehaven Bransty heading the diverted 6C53 Crewe–Sellafield flasks on 20 May 2011.

Immaculately turned out 'Western' Class 52 diesel-hydraulic D1015 *Western Champion* pilots Brush Type 4 D1755 (Class 47 No. 47773) on the 1Z53 Carlisle–Tyseley charter, climbing away from Currock Junction through Cummersdale and on via the Cumbrian Coast line on Saturday 21 September 2013.

In stunning autumnal light, Deltic 55022 *Royal Scots Grey* made a splendid sight and sound powering away from the Border City, captured crossing the River Eden at Etterby, heading a Crewe–Edinburgh charter on 6 November 2010.

It seems as though the sun follows this iconic first-generation Class 55 Deltic. 55022 *Royal Scots Grey* passes Wigton heading a Compass Tours charter from Liverpool to Newcastle on 30 August 2010.

Western Class 52 diesel-hydraulic D1015 *Western Champion* is way off its home territory, fighting the climb up to Shap summit between Greenholme and Scout Green on 31 July 2010.

Above: On Saturday 6 July 2013, DRS 37425 and 20303 negotiate the tight radius of the Carlisle freight line between Currock and Bog junctions, passing Rome Street Gasworks, working the diverted 6K73 Sellafield–Crewe Coal Sidings service, the PFA wagons and container destined for the Berkeley railhead on the following day.

Below: In dappled low winter sunlight, DRS 37688 *Kingmoor TMD* passes Dalston Hall in Cummersdale, heading the 6C42 Sellafield–Kingmoor acid tanks on 5 January 2011.

DBS 66024 heading a well-loaded 6C48 Workington Docks–Carlisle Yard intermodal at Crofton on 27 March 2012. During December 2012 this long-standing railfreight traffic, consistent during the years of railway privatisation, sadly came to an end.

On 12 April 2011, DBS 66164 stands at the head of the 6C48 Workington Docks–Carlisle Yard, comprising intermodal containers for Teesport. Following discharge, the kaolin 'bullet tanks' will be collected on a separate diagram, the 6C69 (Fridays only) working. Behind in one of the port berths is the BNFL ship *Pacific Osprey*.

On 3 March 2010, the Maryport–Workington Floodex shuttle service had DRS 37423 *Spirit of the Lakes* working at the south end of the 'top and tail' formation. The veteran Class 37/4 is seen powering away from the temporary station built on the north side of the River Derwent at Workington.

DRS 47832 *Solway Princess* gets into its stride departing from Workington in charge of an afternoon Floodex shuttle service to Maryport on 19 April 2010.

DRS 47832 *Solway Princess*, with 47501 *Craftsman* at the rear, runs into Workington station to form a Floodex shuttle service to Maryport on 19 April 2010. The cast iron former station roof supports were removed shortly after this. Along with the removal of some of the centre road track removal, this once bustling station area quickly became significantly rationalised.

On 19 April 2010, DRS 47832 *Solway Princess* accelerates away from Workington heading the 1.35 p.m. shuttle service to Maryport. This was a Local Authority/Network Rail/DRS-sponsored community relief service following the flooding, enabling residents living and working north of the River Derwent to go about their everyday business, the railway bridge providing the only direct means of connection between each side of the River Derwent at the time.

With a good covering of snow on the Lakeland Fells behind, DRS 47790 *Galloway Princess* heads a Maryport–Workington shuttle approaching Workington Main on 2 March 2010.

DRS 47501 *Craftsman* runs into Workington station, passing the delightful platform-end Workington Main signalbox, heading a return Floodex shuttle from Maryport on 19 April 2010.

Above: DRS 57012 with a Maryport shuttle Floodex special service at Workington station on 2 March 2010.

Below: DRS 47832 *Solway Princess* skirts the Solway at Flimby heading the 12.20 Workington–Maryport shuttle service on 20 April 2010, following the aftermath of the tragic floods in Cumbria. DRS possess a passenger operating licence and during 2012 also ran a pilot scheme for weekday commuter passenger services between Carlisle and Sellafield.

The NORM low-level radioactive material (Naturally Occurring Radioactive Material) in ISO containers is transferred from the Port of Workington to DRS for onward shipment to the Drigg Repository on 6 May 2003. 20301 *Max Joule 1958–1999* waits at the Port rail boundary gate as the 1979-built Port Hunslet 0-6-0 diesel hydraulic locomotive stands attached to the seven PFA wagons and six ISO containers.

The flagship of the DBS Class 66 fleet, 66001, with Driver Adrian Nichols of Carlisle depot at the controls, heads the 6C48 Workington Docks–Carlisle Yard empty kaolin 'bullet tanks' near Crofton on Friday 7 June 2013. General Motors built all 250 of the EWS Class 66 locomotives at their works at Ontario, in south-east Canada. Initially just 66001 and 66002 were built, the frames being laid on 18 May 1997. On 23 March 1998, 66001 was officially handed over to the EWS Chairman, Ed Burkhardt, at Ontario. After fifteen years of unsung service for EWS and DBS, the flagship locomotive of the fleet received its major overhaul and repaint into the striking red DBS livery, emerging from the paint shop in April 2013 and instantly becoming a celebrity. It was good to see this fleet member on the Maryport & Carlisle line, still looking rather smart in its new coat some eight weeks after emerging ex-works.

On a glorious Saturday 12 July 2003, EWS 56081 leaves Workington Yard with the Hoyer containers from Teesport for unloading at Workington Docks, the 6C17 from Carlisle Yard. Class 56 locomotives were regulars on these services right up until their eventual demise with EWS.

On 9 August 2003, EWS 56049, bearing the unique Dutch Transrail branding, propels its FKA intermodal wagons into Workington Docks at Derwent Junction with the Hoyer containers from Teesport.

DRS 37667 and 37611 power up the grade between Braystones and Nethertown on Wednesday 27 March 2013, heading the 6C53 Crewe–Workington Docks containerised low-level radioactive material originating from Bradwell nuclear power station via the Southminster railhead. The Sellafield and Thorpe reprocessing plants loom on the horizon, outlined against the snow-covered Cumbrian mountains.

Cumbria's West Coast has fast become a major national hub, not just for nuclear expertise, but also for low carbon and renewable energy generation, ranging from offshore wind, tidal and wave to biomass, anaerobic digestion and energy from waste. Rather appropriately, DRS 37611 and 37667 in top and tail formation were captured skirting the Solway coastline near Flimby, dwarfed by some of the many wind turbines that have mushroomed in Cumbria in recent years, both on and off shore. The two half-height ISO containers were conveying low-level radioactive waste, the result of electricity generation at Bradwell nuclear power station. The top and tail formation was to effect a turn-around at Maryport in order to gain access to the up line on to Sellafield, the only operational move now possible for a southbound working out of Workington Docks. This is yet another example of the short-sightedness of railway infrastructure rationalisation that has taken place over the years.

Having deposited seven half-height ISO containers at Workington Port for onward road transport to Lillyhall, DRS 37667 and 37611 skirt the sea wall at Parton on their return journey from Workington Docks to Sellafield, with two containers remaining for onward transfer to the Drigg low-level radioactive waste repository. The PFA four-wheel container wagons are fitted with adaptor frames to allow the carriage of these ISO containers. The original pulverised fly ash and coal containers had insets on the bases to permit flush fitment on the frames over the protruding wheelsets.

DRS 20309 and 20305 are in top and tail formation at Parton sea wall on Thursday 6 June 2013, forming a Workington Docks–Sellafield empty PFA container wagon move after depositing at Workington Docks the low level waste half-height ISO containers originating from the Berkeley railhead in Gloucestershire.

DRS 47501 *Craftsman* passes Dalston station and the BP fuel tanker railhead, heading the Carlisle–Leicester via Cumbrian Coast Route leg of a Rail-Blue charter on 25 August 2010.

In a totally unexpected burst of sunlight, DRS 47810 *Peter Bath MBE 1927–2006* rounds the curve on the jointed track of the Maryport & Carlisle line at Blackwell Hall, heading the 1Z47 07.50 Whitehaven–Blackpool DRS/CFM charity charter on Saturday 31 August 2013.

The non-standard livery of WCRC 57601 at least didn't clash with the paintwork of the delightful 1843-built Maryport & Carlisle water tower at the former Curthwaite station while heading the 1Z70 Brighouse–Carlisle 'Cumbrian Mountain Express' on 28 September 2011. The ivy had also been removed from the overbridge to reveal the wonderful architectural quality of the Cumbrian red sandstone abutments. Curthwaite station, opened in 1843, was closed entirely during 1958. This 'body snatcher' locomotive began its career out-shopped from Brush Works at Loughborough as D1759 in August 1964, first being allocated to Tinsley TMD. It subsequently carried numbers 47165, 47590 and was finally 47825 in Inter City livery before being withdrawn from service prior to conversion at Brush's Loughborough works to the prototype Class 57.

WCRC 57313, still bearing the pleasing Arriva Trains blue livery, heads the 1Z62 Milton Keynes–Carlisle (via the Cumbrian Coast) Statesman charter on Saturday 14 April 2013, seen passing the former Maryport & Carlisle Railway's Crofton station. Located less than a mile from Curthwaite station, Crofton station was built to serve the adjacent Crofton Estate, seen to the right of the image, but was closed in 1954.

DRS 37667 and 37688 *Kingmoor TMD* take the freight avoiding lines at Bog Junction, Carlisle, and dip under the St Nicholas road bridge, heading the diverted 6K73 Sellafield–Crewe flasks on 11 May 2011. The opposite side of this bridge was once a very popular strategic location for observing trains when all the freight avoiding lines were open.

Veteran DRS 'Growlers' 37087 *Keighley and Worth Valley 40th Anniversary 1968–2008* and 37194 negotiate the overgrown freight route at Bog Junction, Carlisle, heading the 6M60 Seaton–Sellafield flask working on 8 August 2011, the only regular daylight working over this route, and in this direction only, once per week.

The sole-surviving main line 'split-box' Class 37, DRS 37087 *Keighley and Worth Valley Railway 40th Anniversary 1968–2008* (with 37667 on the rear in the usual top and tail operational formation required for the Heysham workings), approaches Bog Junction on 14 April 2011. This was the 6C52 Heysham–Sellafield flasks, diverted via Carlisle as a result of the closure of the Arnside Bridge for essential repair work. 37087 was withdrawn from service in June 2012 and was sent for disposal at Booth's scrapyard at Rotherham in February 2013, following component recovery at Barrow Hill, an ignominious end for a onetime celebrity locomotive.

DRS 57011 and 57002 traverse the freight connecting line between Bog Junction and Currock Junction, heading the 6M60 Seaton–Sellafield flasks on 5 April 2012. Rome Street Gasworks, the Citadel and Carlisle station dominate the background scene.

Striking DBS-liveried Class 67 No. 67018 *Keith Heller* attracts the attention of enthusiasts at Carlisle station with the 1Z69 Rail-Blue charter from Harlow on 27 April 2011.

In falling snow on 1 December 2010, DBS 67030 heads a Compass Tours Worcester–Edinburgh charter northwards from the Border City, crossing the Eden river bridge.

A perfectly timed burst of autumnal sunlight catches DBS 67005 *Royal Messenger*, heading the 2.48 p.m. return Rail-Blue charters special via the Cumbrian Coast line, on the Maryport and Carlisle section at Dockray near Wigton on 30 October 2010.

The 1Z20 Glasgow Central–Southampton Western Docks 'Cruisex' with DBS 67026 *Diamond Jubilee* looking smart up front, despite the damp and overcast conditions, effortlessly accelerates away from its brief stop at Carlisle station, just after 7.30 a.m. on 30 June 2012.

Stobart Rail-liveried EWS 92017 *Bart the Engine*, a one-time regular for the service when contracted with EWS, heads the 4S43 Rugby–Mossend across the frozen River Esk at Mossband on 21 December 2010.

In sub-zero temperatures on 20 December 2010, Freightliner Intermodal 86604 and 86621 head the 4S52 Crewe–Coatbridge across the Eden river bridge, north of Carlisle.

Above: Performing a role for which the class were originally designed, DBS 67019 is heading a Shieldmuir–Warrington pre-Christmas postal extra at Mossband on 21 December 2010.

Below: A Glasgow Central–London Euston Virgin Pendolino glides across the frozen Esk Valley at Mossband on 22 December 2010.

Tackling the climb to Shap summit, 92017 *Bart the Engine* heads the 4S43 Rugby–Mossend Tesco 'Less CO2' intermodal at Greenholme on 24 July 2010.

The minor road, originally providing access to Scout Green level crossing and the well-known signal box of the steam era, is now sadly overgrown and almost a running stream in the rain of 11 May 2012, as DBS 92031 effortlessly passes by heading the 4S43 Daventry–Mossend 'Tesco less CO2' service. By this time bearing the striking DBS corporate livery, the locomotive previously carried the name *The Institute of Logistics and Transport*.

Above: DBS 92012 *Thomas Hardy* heads the 4S43 Rugby–Mossend 'Tesco Less CO2' intermodal through unforgiving rain near Southwaite on 13 May 2011.

Below: Regular locomotive 92017 *Bart the Engine* climbs the grade at Scout Green, heading the 4S43 Rugby–Mossend Tesco intermodal on 31 July 2010.

A trailing load of eight loaded FNA flask wagons is enough to get any locomotive snarling and the 6C53 from Crewe to Sellafield on 29 April 2011 was no exception. 20303 and 37059 accelerate away from Carlisle through Cummersdale at Blackwell Hall, providing a very pleasing spectacle.

Situated where North Lancashire meets South Cumbria, the Arnside & Silverdale Area, declared in 1972 and covering only 29 square miles is one of the smallest AONBs, in the country. Adding an unexpected splash of colour to the delightful scene on the edge of Morecambe Bay is Loadhaul-liveried 37698, heading an afternoon flask train working to Sellafield near Silverdale in July 1997, during the early and indeed short period of EWS ownership, just before DRS over all nuclear-associated rail operations on the national network, initially based from their headquarters and maintenance facility at Sellafield. Of note are the two barrier wagons each side of the four FNA wagons and flasks, and the brakevan, such a formation being dispensed with under DRS custodianship. A higher running speed of the FNAs was also eventually permitted, once approval was granted by Derby RTC after a number of modifications and rigorous tests had been undertaken, thereby offering enhanced pathing opportunities on the busy West Coast Main Line.

With a threatening sky over Carlisle, DRS 57007 and 57003 head a single flask through Wigton station, the 6M60 Seaton–Sellafield on 14 April 2011.

With the sound of curlew calling overhead, the tranquillity of a Cummersdale mid-summer's evening is momentarily broken and a crow is disturbed as DRS *Spirit of the Lakes* and 37409 *Lord Hinton* growl towards Currock Junction just before 9.00 p.m. with three FNA wagons and flasks in tow, the 6C46 7.11 p.m. Sellafield–Carlisle Kingmoor on Wednesday 16 June 2013.

WCRC 47760 is seen at the head of the coaching stock at Carlisle forming The Caledonian charter, the 1Z24 from Glasgow to Tyseley on 28 May 2012. Delivered new from BR Crewe Works to Toton (16A) TMD in September 1964 as D1614, it has subsequently borne numbers 47036, 47562, 47672, 47760, three names (*Sir William Burrell*, *Restless* and *Ribblehead Viaduct*) and six different liveries during its fifty-year career.

A brief 'Brush interlude' when Brush Type 2 No. 31106 and Brush Type 4 No. 47760 make a chance encounter at Carlisle station on 28 May 2012. 31106 was delivered new from the Brush Traction Falcon Works at Loughborough as D5524 in March 1959 and first allocated to Stratford (30A) depot. An amazing main line survivor, looking good in the BR rail blue livery.

For a limited period after their initial introduction into service the PowerHaul Class 70 was trialled on Anglo-Scottish intermodal services, but such deployment was to be short-lived. 70003 heads the 4M74 14.01 Coatbridge–Crewe Basford Hall through Carlisle in the rain on 28 October 2010.

Unique Malcolm-liveried DRS 66412, on loan to Freightliner at this time, pauses for a crew change at Carlisle while heading 4Z87 Coatbridge–Crewe intermodal on 9 December 2010. 66412 was subsequently leased by Freightliner after DRS terminated their contract and it is now working in Poland.

This book would be incomplete without a view incorporating Direct Rail Services' Kingmoor TMD. The peace and quiet at 6.35 a.m. on a wet May morning is disturbed by the thrash of English Electric veterans 20302 and 37259 as the driver of 6C22 Kingmoor–Sellafield flasks powers up after clearing the exit from the depot. Class 20 No. 20302 started out life as D8084 in October 1961 and was a regular visitor to Kingmoor steam motive power depot in the 1960s. The former depot site is now the Sidings Nature Reserve, seen to the right of the tracks in the photograph. The Class 37, No. 37259, started out as D6959 in January 1965 initially allocated to Tinsley depot.

With a Condor headboard affixed to 47810 *Peter Bath MBE 1927–2006*, DRS driver Mike Wylie powers away from Carlisle Kingmoor Depot and across the Eden river bridge with the empty stock from the final contracted DRS Cruise Saver boat train working from Southampton to Glasgow, which ran on the previous day.

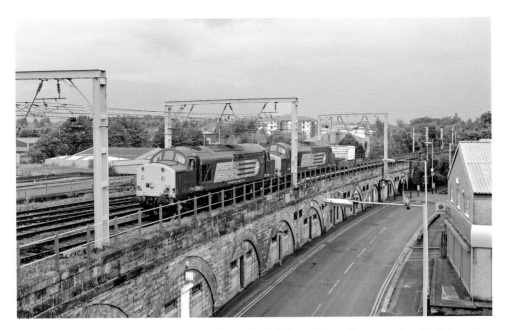

DRS 37604 and 37601 trundle across the arches at English Damside, on the approach to Carlisle station, heading a single flask, the 6C22 6.45 a.m. Kingmoor–Sellafield on 15 July 2010.

With three coal trains having just been stacked up on the freight lines north of Carlisle due to network congestion, the driver of DRS 37229, anxious to maintain the company's punctuality target with the customer, leans out of his cab to see if the train in the next section south on the freight lines is underway. The 6M22 Hunterston–Sellafield flask train is seen in DRS Kingmoor depot yard on 14 June 2012. The Class 37 is flanked on depot by 47818 and 57011.

Seen from the stone causeway of the River Ehen at Sellafield, DRS Class 37/4 37423 *Spirit of the Lakes* waits to take up its return diagram to Carlisle, the 2T21 4.48 Sellafield–Carlisle trial commuter service on 15 February 2012. The rather corroded semaphore signal gantry, exposed unforgivingly to the raw elements of the Irish Sea, will soon be replaced under the protracted Cumbrian Coast resignalling scheme currently ongoing.

A busy scene at Sellafield station yard on 15 February 2012 with 57004 and 57007 stabled in the up head shunt, 37423 *Spirit of the Lakes* at the head of the stock for the return 2T21 service to Carlisle and Northern Rail's 156481 approaching the station, forming a Carlisle service. In the DRS compound behind the Sellafield site security fence is an assortment of nuclear flask wagons and flasks, as well as an internal shunting locomotive.

DRS 20305 and 20309 top and tail the 6Z45 Workington Docks–Sellafield–Crewe low level waste half-height ISO containers at St Bees on Tuesday 4 June 2013.

The 6C53 Crewe–Sellafield flasks, with 57007 and 57004 in charge, powers through Bootle on 8 February 2012, leaving an exhaust trail hovering in its wake.

With rain falling over the Solway Firth beyond Carlisle, GB Railfreight's 66737 *Lesia* rounds the curve at Great Corby, heading the diverted 6E45 Fort William–North Blyth (Alcan) aluminium tanks on Wednesday 29 May 2013. The sun's position would be right into the camera lens at this time of day, just after 6.00 p.m., but a brighter spot in the clouds behind the photographer fortunately illuminated the scene against the dark background.

In rapidly failing light at 9.00 p.m., DBS 92031 crosses the Eden river bridge at Etterby, Carlisle, with the very late running (almost twelve hours) 4S43 Daventry–Mossend Tesco intermodal service on 29 June 2012. Usually a full train, the empty container carrying wagons towards the rear of the train indicated that the more timely products for delivery had probably already made their journey by road before loading commenced at the terminal.

Heralding the start of the Railhead Treatment Train season, Direct Rail Services 37423 *Spirit of the Lakes* approaches Kingmoor Depot in pouring rain with a rake of Network Rail water jet tanks, the 6Z31 from York on 20 September 2012.

The low golden sunlight belies the fact that the temperature is barely above freezing at Wetheral Plains on the Tyne Valley line as the mist gradually forms and the temperature drops further. DRS 66432 heads the late-running 6Z11 12.40 Kingmoor Sidings–York on 11 December 2012, comprising the Carlisle-based sets of railhead treatment jet wash tanks being returned to Network Rail at York upon completion of the Carlisle-based 2012 railhead treatment season.

Disturbing the peace of the Eden Valley, DRS 37682 and 37229 *Jonty Jarvis* power away from Corby Gates level crossing, Great Corby, heading the 6E44 Kingmoor Depot–Seaton flasks on 18 June 2012 – two classic DRS 37s in a location that is only suitably sunlit for this working in the high summer.

Freightliner Heavyhaul 66524 heading Drax Power Station–Ravenstruther coal loading point empty coal hoppers along the Tyne Valley route at Great Corby on 9 May 2011.

A pair of named DRS Class 20/3s, 20301 *Max Joule 1958–1999* and 20305 *Gresty Bridge*, make a rare appearance on the 6E44 Kingmoor Depot–Seaton flask working on Monday 11 June 2012. The pair is seen here leaning the sharp curve through the splendid Wetheral station, with its restored North Eastern Railway footbridge providing safe pedestrian access to this established public right of way over the Tyne Valley line.

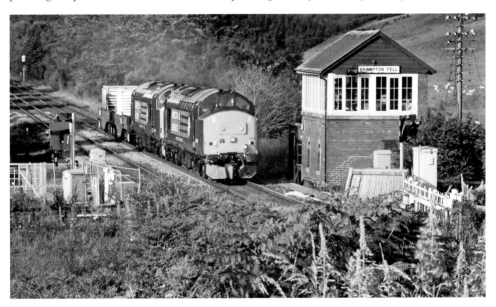

The striking rosebay willowherb (fireweed) flowers offer foreground mid-summer interest as DRS 37419 and 37682 power past Brampton Fell signal box at 8.00 a.m. on Tuesday 31 July 2012, heading the 6E44 nuclear flasks from Sellafield (via Kingmoor depot) to Seaton. Brampton Fell was one of two boxes erected in 1918 to control new goods loops (independent lines in NER terminology) on the Newcastle & Carlisle route. The box at the other end of the loops was rather curiously called Hell Beck, but this closed during cutbacks in the 1920s. In more recent years these sidings also became redundant but the box and its 20-lever McKenzie & Holland frame survives as a simple block post controlling the adjoining level crossing on the B6413 road. The crossing was equipped with boom gates until twelve days after this image was taken. These were full length gates running on rubber-tyred wheels operated by electric motors. Work at this time was in hand for their replacement and Babcock Rail engineers had just arrived to continue with this work, some of the new equipment already being installed and visible in this scene.

On a perfect early autumn morning, Saturday 28 September 2013, WCRC 'no-heat' 47245 heads the 1Z43 05.22 Linlithgow–Grange-over-sands through Cummersdale at Blackwell, a rare outing for a Class 47/0 on a passenger charter.

47580 *County of Essex* eases the 1Z62 Lincoln–Carlisle 'Lakeland Moorlander' charter across Petteril Bridge, Carlisle, on Saturday 25 May 2013, marking the completion of its transit over the Settle–Carlisle section of the charter and reaching its destination several minutes early. Introduced to BR traffic on 1 September 1964 as D1762, this veteran is closely approaching half a century of mainline service at the time of writing.

The 1Z25 Glasgow and Edinburgh–York 'Northern Belle' on Sunday 23 September was routed via Carlisle. DRS 47828 rounds the curve out of Carlisle station to take the Tyne Valley route to Newcastle and onward to York, the onset of autumn and the leaf-fall season very evident here.

DRS 47501 *Craftsman* and 47831 *Solway Princess* climb the grade heading the 1Z24 Inverness–Salisbury Pathfinder Tours charter at Southwaite on 25 April 2011.

Left: DRS 66428 heads a well-laden 4S44 Daventry–Coatbridge intermodal service, snaking past Shapbeck Bridge on 15 August 2013.

Below: One of only three red DBS Class 66s at the time, 66152 *Derek Holmes Railway Operator* trundles over the Esk river bridge at Mossband, returning spoil to Carlisle yard following overnight lineside drainage work at overbridge 316 at Ruthwell on the G&SW route. This was the 6K15 Annan–Carlisle Yard Engineer's diagram on Sunday 17 June 2012.

The weather is somewhat different over Kendal and across the border into North Lancashire as Freightliner Heavyhaul 66547 heads the 4C20 Fiddlers Ferry–Carlisle New Yard empty coal hoppers north down the West Coast Main Line at Lambrigg on Saturday 1 March 2014, a point where the railway curiously turns and heads due east for a short stretch. This was the location of the tragic Grayrigg Pendolino derailment that occurred here on 23 February 2007.

As the humidity rises and the clouds start to form, heralding an impending thunderstorm, DRS 37602 and 37606 make their own thunder and just catch the last of the sun's rays disappearing behind the encroaching black clouds as they power away from Carlisle heading the 4M82 Coatbridge–Daventry intermodal on Monday 22 July 2013. They are substituting for the normal Class 66/4s diagrammed for this train and turning back the clock to the earlier days of DRS Class 37-hauled intermodal services on the WCML.

With a colourful rake of coaching stock in tow, DRS 47805 hurries across the Anglo-Scottish border at Gretna heading the 1Z80 Southampton Eastern Docks–Glasgow Central Cruisex boat train at a photographic location very much favoured by the late Bishop Eric Treacy. It is now sadly overgrown, but the border crossing signs are still visible, and indeed a topical feature in the year of publication of this book.

Freightliner Heavyhaul 70005 makes slow progress heading the 6C16 Crewe–Carlisle engineers' train past Shap Wells on Wednesday 22 May 2013, seemingly a rather mundane task for such a powerful and modern class of locomotive – surely not its original deployment envisaged when on the drawing board. The Shap Wells Hotel, adjacent to this location on the WCML, was a favourite overnight spot for some well-known railway photographers around half a century ago, including Bishop Eric Treacy, Derek Cross and Ivo Peters.

On 29 March 2012, DRS 37603 and 37606 pass the former Thursby Mill (now a private dwelling) at Curthwaite in charge of the 6M60 Seaton–Sellafield diagram, with two FNA wagons and flasks in tow.

Against a backdrop of threatening skies over the Border City, an up Virgin service comprising two Voyager 5-car sets, with unit 221142 leading, leans to the curve at milepost 66 near Carleton, south of Carlisle, on 15 June 2013.

The first daylight appearance of a Colas Class 56 on the WCML over Shap: the 6J37 12.44 Carlisle Yard–Chirk (Kronospan) loaded timber on Saturday 22 September 2012, with 56094 up front, getting underway after being looped at Shap Summit in order to allow an up Virgin service to pass.

The 6K05 Carlisle Yard–Crewe Basford Hall departmental service can always be relied upon to provide variety in the rolling stock, if not traction. The movement on 29 March 2012 provided a pleasing, colourful but uniform consist. With an enthusiastic acknowledgement from the Carlisle DBS driver, 66019 powers past Duncowfold on a glorious spring day. The surviving telegraph posts are an interesting feature along this short stretch of the Settle–Carlisle line.

On 27 February 2004, EWS 60057 heads the 9.58 a.m. Workington Yard–Carlisle Corus rails, near former mine workings north of Maryport at Crosby, a regular diagram for EWS Tugs during this period.

On 25 February 2004, EWS 56094 *Eggborough Power Station* rounds the curve through Wigton heading the 11.00 a.m. Workington Docks–Kingmoor Yard–Tees Yard EWS network service comprising two empty kaolin bullet tanks and FKA intermodal flats, some with Hoyer containers.

EWS Class 37s 37405 and 37408 *Loch Rannoch*, on hire to Arriva Trains, top and tail a Leeds–Carlisle morning service near Cotehill on 11 February 2004.

47580 *County of Essex* heads the 1Z79 Carlisle–Swindon 'Statesman' at Low Cotehill on the Settle–Carlisle line on 14 May 2011. 47580 is owned by the Stratford 47 Group, a group formed in 2001 with the aim of preserving a Class 47 that was allocated to the former Stratford Depot in London and was once a familiar sight on the former Eastern Region of BR in the 1970s and 1980s.

DBS 66149 heads the 6L49 Carlisle North Yard–Leyland in the rain on Saturday 8 February 2014, emerging from the 325-yard-long Armathwaite Tunnel into Baron Wood.

With the lineside rosebay willowherb looking at its best just before going to seed and with the splendour of the Eden Valley as a backdrop, Freightliner 66554 heads the 6M32 Killoch–Ratcliffe coal diagram via the Settle and Carlisle line near Dry Beck on 27 July 2011.

In failing light DRS 'Northern Belle'-liveried 47832 *Solway Princess*, with Driver Mike Wylie at the controls, powers through the closed Cumwhinton station on 15 December 2011 heading the return leg of the 'Northern Belle' charter, the 1Z35 to Darlington and Newcastle via Leeds.

With no appreciable rainfall experienced for several weeks and consistently cold north-easterly winds during that period, the green shoots of spring had yet to appear in the Eden Valley, and even the grass had taken on a parched appearance more akin to an arid environment totally alien to the British Isles. Driver Mike Wylie of DRS 37607 and 37402 gives a friendly wave and acknowledges on the horn as the pair growl south over the Settle–Carlisle line at Duncowfold on Monday 1 April 2013, heading the 1Z36 9.44 a.m. Dumbarton–Exeter St David's 'Pathfinder Tours Easter Highlander charter.

With the distinctive 'Helm' hanging over the northern Pennines, WCRC 47804 heads the 1Z63 Skegness–Newcastle via Carlisle charter at Duncowfold in stunning conditions on 11 December 2010.

In a delightful early summer setting, DRS 37419 *Carl Haviland* propels inspection saloon coach *Caroline* past the closed Cumwhinton station, heading a Carlisle–Derby RTC move via the Settle–Carlisle line on 17 June 2013. The vehicle *Caroline* was originally built in 1958 at Eastleigh Works as type AZA trailer restaurant buffet car (TRB) S60755, for a British Rail Class 203 diesel-electric Hastings multiple-unit, No. 1036, until withdrawal during 1964. These 'Hasting Units' had a narrow body profile for working through tunnels on the Hastings Line, and this is the reason for the continued narrow width of *Caroline*. The saloon carriage is notable for being used as the British Royal Train between London Waterloo and Romsey for the first part of the honeymoon trip following the wedding of Charles, Prince of Wales, and Lady Diana Spencer on 29 July 1981. One year later on 28 May 1982 *Caroline* was the transport for Pope John Paul II's visit to the United Kingdom between Gatwick Airport and London Victoria station. Additionally, *Caroline* formed the first standard gauge passenger service into the Channel Tunnel on 22 October 1992, leaving from Waterloo International railway station and propelled by 73112 *University of Kent* into the tunnel.

DRS 37423 *Spirit of the Lakes* crosses the River Caldew in Cummersdale in charge of the 2Z02 Preston–Preston via the Cumbrian Coast line charter by Derby Railway Technical Centre on Friday 20 September 2013. It is assumed that a jolly nice day out was had by all!

Recently out-shopped 37409 *Lord Hinton* and 37059 growl through Cummersdale, having just crossed the River Caldew bridge, heading the diverted 6C53 Crewe–Sellafield flasks on 5 May 2011.

DRS 20304 and 20302 accelerate away from the Border City through Cummersdale and across the recently renovated Caldew river bridge, heading the late-running 6M22 Hunterston–Sellafield on Tuesday 4 June 2013.

Immaculate DRS 47832 *Solway Princess* is powering away from the Border City of Carlisle heading the 1Z22 5.51 a.m. Crewe–Edinburgh 'Northern Belle' across the Eden river bridge at Etterby on Friday 23 August 2013. The Brush Type 4 was delivered new from BR Crewe Works to Swansea Landore (87E) depot in August 1964 as D1610, and it remained loyal to the Western Region throughout most of its BR career.

DRS 37602 and 37603 speed the 5Z18 Derby RTC–Mossend, with test car *Hermes*, across the Esk river bridge at Mossband on 11 April 2011.

Extremely careful observation of the local tide table in the Kent Estuary was made before attempting this photograph! Class 55 Deltic 55019 *Royal Highland Fusilier* heading a prestigious Liverpool–Barrow 'Northern Belle' VSOE charter train across the Arnside viaduct on 6 October 2000. This was over a decade before total refurbishment of the viaduct commenced. During the protracted refurbishment all Sellafield freight services were routed via north Cumbria, consequently providing a number of photographic opportunities not normally available and featured elsewhere in this book. This Deltic entered BR service as D9019 during December 1961, being based at Haymarket depot in Edinburgh. The last member of the classes to be named, the ceremony took place at Glasgow Central station in September 1965. It was renumbered under the TOPs scheme to 55019 in November 1973 and was one of only five members of the class to undergo the extensive Heavy General Repairs (HGR) overhaul at Doncaster works. It worked its last BR train on 31 December 1981, hauling the Aberdeen–York service between Edinburgh and York, also the final BR Deltic-hauled service train. Withdrawn the same day due to it being surplus to requirements after over twenty years of active service, it was purchased for preservation in the same year by The Deltic Preservation Society (DPS) and acquired a main line certificate in 1999, after considerable work undertaken at Barrow Hill depot.

As a result of engineering works on the ECML north of Newcastle-upon-Tyne, the 6S45 North Blyth–Fort William was diverted via the Tyne Valley and Carlisle on 1 September 2011. GB Railfreight's 66733 approaches Etterby Bridge with the laden alumina silo tanks.

DRS 37229 *Jonty Jarvis* and 37218 head the 6K73 Sellafield–Crewe across the Eskmeals Viaduct on 21 July 2011.

On 6 May 2003 a shipment of naturally occurring radioactive material (NORM) was moved from Workington Docks to the Drigg Repository for long-term storage. The half-height ISOs contain low-level radioactive rock extracted from the sea bed as a result of drilling in the North Sea for oil. In top and tail formation (with 20304 out of view on the rear), DRS 20301 *Max Joule 1958–1999* skirts Harrington Harbour with six ISOs loaded on PFA wagons.

DRS 20304 and 20301 skirt the Solway Firth at Parton on the morning of 6 May 2003 with empty PFA wagons from Sellafield to Workington Dock for the collection of containerised low level radioactive (NORM) material.

The spectacular but exposed location at Redness Point, just north of Whitehaven, with DRS 66423 and 66424 in top and tail formation with two flasks, the diverted 6C51 from Sellafield to Heysham on 12 May 2011.

The diverted 6K73 Sellafield–Crewe flask (via Carlisle Bog Junction) trundling along the sea wall at Tanyard Bay near Parton on 2 May 2011.

Apparent super power for one flask, but in effect a loco transfer move with the Class 37 dead, but still 4,960 horsepower for the driver to play with, two locomotives being a contractual requirement for the fuel rod reprocessing services serving Sellafield and the nuclear power stations. DRS 66428, 66431 and 37229 head the diverted 6C53 Crewe–Sellafield past the River Caldew in Cummersdale on 4 May 2011.

With the Higginson and Shaddon Mills, Dixons chimney, Carlisle castle and the cathedral all visible on the skyline, DRS 37409 *Lord Hinton* and 37087 *Keighley and Worth Valley Railway 40th Anniversary 1968–2008* power away from Currock Junction, leaving a trail of exhaust fumes, in charge of the late running 6C53 Crewe–Sellafield nuclear flasks on 23 June 2011.

DRS 20303 and 20309 pass the BP private sidings at Dalston in charge of the 6C22 6.45 Kingmoor–Sellafield flasks on 27 May 2011.

DRS 57008 *Telford International Railfreight Park June 2009* and 57009 make easy work of a single flask, the 6M60 Seaton–Sellafield, as they accelerate away from Currock Junction, Carlisle, at Blackwell Hall on 30 May 2011.

Waste from the 1870s ironworks established on the sea shore at Parton is still evident on the shore line in this view of DRS 37604 and 37218 heading the 6K73 Sellafield–Crewe at Providence Bay, Parton, on 12 April 2011. Traffic to and from Sellafield was routed via Bog Junction at Carlisle for several months during the rebuilding of Arnside viaduct.

With heavy rain falling across the Solway Firth on 12 April 2011, DRS 37218 and 37604 head a lightly loaded 6C53 Crewe–Sellafield flask train at Salterbeck, diverted via Carlisle Bog Junction. Clearly there wasn't a pot of gold to be found at the bottom of this rainbow, for the developers of the former Workington Steelworks site to the right in this scene had still not made any progress in finding sufficient interest for the reuse of the land by 2014.

Above: On 26 July 2003, recently out-shopped DRS 37038, with 20901, skirts the Solway Firth in the rain at Tanyard Bay on Saturday 26 July 2003 with two flasks from Sellafield for Kingmoor.

Below: DRS 57009 and 57008 are seen working a Sellafield–Crewe support coach transfer move near Curthwaite on 6 April 2011.

On Friday 7 June 2013, DRS 57011 and 57007 (with 37194 DIT) power through Cummersdale at Blackwell Hall, the 6C22 6.40 Carlisle Kingmoor–Sellafield nuclear flask working, ex-6M60 from Seaton the previous afternoon.

The low morning sun glints on the front of DRS 37606, working in tandem with 37603 as they round the tight curve and power away from Corby Gates level crossing on the Tyne Valley line, working the 6E44 Kingmoor–Seaton flasks on 29 March 2012.

DRS 37423 *Spirit of the Lakes* (with 37261 on the rear) erupts out of London Road tunnel as it leaves a wet Border City heading a DRS Kingmoor Open Day Special, the 1Z12 from Carlisle to Newcastle-upon-Tyne and return on Saturday 17 August 2013. It looks as though great fun was had by all, including the traincrew!

As a precursor to the impending commuter passenger trial services between Carlisle–Sellafield–Barrow, DRS 37610 *T. S. (Ted) Cassady 14.5.61–6.4.08* worked a 12.45 5Z20 Sellafield–Carlisle Kingmoor crew training diagram on 29 September 2011, photographed near Crofton on the Maryport and Carlisle section of the Cumbrian Coast line. The loco was dedicated to the late Ted Cassady, who was Professional Head of Engineering at DRS from its inception. A larger than life character, he is very sadly missed in the company.

DRS 66425 and 66303 (the latter still bearing the Fastline decals shortly after acquisition by DRS) power away from Currock Junction through Cummersdale on 7 April 2011, with five flasks forming the 6C53 from Crewe to Sellafield.

An idyllic scene: the diverted 6K73 Sellafield–Crewe flask train captured trundling through the lush meadows of Cummersdale and passing the River Caldew, with DRS 20303 and 37688 doing the honours on 16 June 2011.

DRS 37194 near Crofton at the head of the 6C42 Sellafield–Carlisle Yard empty caustic soda bogie tank wagons on 9 September 2010. Released from English Electric Robert Stephenson & Hawthorns works as D6894 in March 1964 and first allocated to Landore depot, it was eventually withdrawn from service in January 1999 and acquired by Harry Needle Rail at Barrow Hill. Purchased by DRS in February 2005 and relatively unmodified, it has proved to be a favourite locomotive for main line charters, also appearing at some heritage railway galas.

An incredible chance meeting captured by the camera: DRS 37682, working the 6C42 Sellafield–Carlisle Yard chemical tanks, crossing with 66417, 66422, 37667 and 37087 heading away from Currock Junction towards Sellafield through Cummersdale with the diverted 6C53 Crewe–Sellafield flask working on 6 April 2011.

Dwarfed by the Stead McAlpin textile mill chimney in Cummersdale, DRS 37419 Carl Haviland and 37612 head the 6M22 Hunterston–Sellafield Reprocessing Plant flask working on Tuesday 30 April 2013, conveying a fine portrait of Cumbrian industry still remaining in the twenty-first century.

DBS 66027, with a consignment of kaolin in five 'bullet' tanks, nods up and down on the jointed and severely dipping track as it heads away from Carlisle through Cummersdale, heading the 6C68 Carlisle Yard–Workington Docks on 23 March 2012.

During 2013 DRS signed a contract with Network Rail's National Delivery Service (NDS) to provide haulage for some of the company's fleet of engineering trains at various locations around the network, providing occasional opportunities such as this diagram, the 6L65 4.10 p.m. Carlisle Yard–Sellafield with 37612 in charge at Blackwell Hall on Saturday 20 April 2013.

DRS 37606 and 37602 (with Malcolm-liveried 66434 in transit to Crewe via Sellafield) head the 6C24 Carlisle Kingmoor TMD–Sellafield acid tankers, which arrived at the depot from Middlesbrough during the previous evening. This was the first and possibly only visit of the 'Malcolm-liveried' Class 66 to the Cumbrian Coast Line. The former Maryport & Carlisle-built goods shed and office still survives (behind the Class 66) and the listed building is now rented out for light industrial use. The factory in the centre of town behind is owned by Innovia, Wigton's principal employer. In 1936 the British New Wrap Co. Ltd was formed in Wigton, Cumbria, and production of cellulose film began at the site, which had previously been a jam-making facility and was then set up to produce 'artificial silk' or Rayon. In 1936 the company changed its name to British Rayophane Ltd. Its main products are labels and graphics, cellophane and Propafilm, bubble-produced BOPP film, substrates for plastic banknotes (currently used for all Australian, New Zealand, Romanian and Vietnamese currencies) and plastic labels, replacing paper labels due to their resistance to tearing, scuffing and water damage.

With the Thorpe Reprocessing Plant dominating the scene overlooking Braystones Beach, DRS 37667 and 37611 undertake a Crewe–Workington Docks low level waste container movement on 27 March 2013.

On 30 July 2013, DRS 37609 and 37605 (with 37608 DIT) power away from Currock Junction through Cummersdale at Blackwell Hall, the 6C53 Crewe–Sellafield via Bog Junction comprising two PFA wagons and a single ISO container of low level radioactive waste loaded the previous day at the Berkeley railhead in Gloucestershire.

In the Lune Gorge the M6 motorway and the West Coast Main Line cling to the lower contours of Whinfell, with the River Lune flowing peacefully deep in the valley. On Saturday 22 September DBS 92035 *Bertoldt Brecht* effortlessly climbs to Tebay and onward to Shap summit with the 'Tesco Less CO2' service, the 4S43 intermodal from Daventry to Mossend.

On a perfect high summer's afternoon WCRC 47760 heads the 1Z73 Carlisle–York 'Waverley' at Stockber on Sunday 5 August 2012, substituting for the booked steam locomotive, *Scots Guardsman*, which was declared a failure at Carlisle following its northbound working from York.

The widely travelled Colas Rail Freight 'Grid' 56094 made its debut under Colas ownership over the Settle–Carlisle line on Monday 1 October 2012 and is seen here rounding the curve on the approach to Kirkby Stephen station heading the 6J37 Carlisle Yard–Chirk diagram, carrying timber predominantly logged in the Kielder Forest and destined to become chipboard for use in kitchen, bedroom and office furniture.

Colas Railfreight's immaculate Class 56 'Grid' 56105 dives into the cutting at Armathwaite Tunnel heading the 6J37 Carlisle Yard–Chirk loaded timber on 20 April 2013.

With a total of 6,500 hp at the disposal of the driver, Colas Railfreight 56105 and 56087 throb up the 1 in 132 grade at Duncowfold, heading the 6J37 Carlisle Yard–Chirk timber on Thursday 11 July 2013. They could certainly be heard coming from a long way off. Five years ago, who would have imagined that such a spectacle would once again become reality on the national network?

A bonus of the light summer evenings is the opportunity to capture the 6S00 Clitheroe–Mossend loaded cement on the renowned Settle–Carlisle route. DB Schenker's 66111 heads a northbound service in the low evening sunshine at Kirkby Stephen on 18 August 2010.

Colas Railfreight's 66850 approaches London Road Junction, Carlisle, passing the former site (to the right) of Cowan's Sheldon crane maker's yard, heading the 6J37 Carlisle Yard–Chirk Kronospan loaded timber via the Settle–Carlisle line on 23 August 2011.

Top: EWS Class 60 'Tug' 60099 *Ben More Assynt*, bearing its pre-privatisation Mainline decals, passes Culgaith crossing heading up loaded coal over the Settle–Carlisle line in July 1998.

Middle: DBS 66114 approaches Birkett Tunnel heading the 6K05 Carlisle Yard–Crewe Basford Hall Engineers' service on Monday 1 October 2012. The latter part of the train comprised one section of the high output ballast cleaning (HOBC) train, which had seen regular use over the previous couple of months on the Tyne Valley line with Class 60s top and tailing the 'jumbo' trains, a qualification in terms of both their tare and trailing length.

Bottom: Just six months after entering traffic, EWS 66107 stands out in this scene, with the stark and foreboding backdrop of Wild Boar Fell dominating. The Kirkby Thore–Drax containerised gypsum empties is approaching Ais Gill summit and the Cumbria/North Yorkshire county boundary on 4 September 1999.

First Great Western 57605 *Totnes Castle* makes an extremely rare appearance in the North, away from Brunel's railway, heading the 5Z57 Crewe–Kilmarnock (Wabtec) empty stock move on Tuesday 24 September 2013, crossing the Eden river bridge north of the Border City.

Undoubtedly the finest array of semaphore signalling surviving on the Settle–Carlisle line today is at Appleby, although the main down gantry has a prominent inclination to the west! The engineers' sidings branching off to the right, at one time providing access to the Warcop branch with its military traffic in latter years, look like a major junction in this view, such is the quality of the track upgrading work recently undertaken. This is hardly surprising, with Appleby now being a strategic engineers' hub for the Settle–Carlisle line. DRS 66432 approaches Appleby station on Wednesday 14 August 2013 heading a short 6K05 Carlisle Yard–Crewe Basford Hall departmental working.

DRS 47853 *Rail Express* tows brand new 68002 *Intrepid* and its eleven trailing coaches across the Eden River Bridge at Etterby. Having just left DRS Kingmoor Depot, this was the first trial loaded test run, on Tuesday 4 February 2014, with a hired-in DBS Class 90 taking over at Carlisle station for the return diagram to Crewe.

The new order in Cumbria: a front-end study of DRS' new Vossloh Class 68 No. 68002 *Intrepid* on the rear of the 5Z70 Crewe–Carlisle Kingmoor empty stock move, seen at Carlisle station on 5 February 2014. The application of worksplates (Vossloh works No. 2680/2013) is a refreshing finishing touch, and they will undoubtedly be much sought after collector's items in many years to come.